CONTENTS

	BOOK DESCRIPTION	1-2
	BOOK INTRODUCTION	3-4
1	WHO IS AN ENTREPRENEUR	5
2	FEARS BEFORE STARTING A BUSINESS	12
3	HOW TO START A BUSINESS	21
4	HOW TO MAKE YOUR BUSINESS SUCCESSFUL	29
	BOOK SUMMARY	36
	ABOUT THE AUTHOR	38

BOOK DESCRIPTION

Need a little push when it comes to turning your dreams into reality?

Is entrepreneurial success the phenomenon you seem to be chasing?

Well, it will be my honor to inform you that you have just taken the first step in a journey that will directly lead you to financial freedom and entrepreneurial success!

This book has been divided into a course of four chapters, and each section will bring to you brand new and enlightening information regarding your way to fulfill your dreams and achieve the best in the entrepreneurial side of the business.

By picking up this guide-book, you have just done yourself a landmark, worthy favor, because from here on out the information you will be receiving not only help you reach heights it will also push you up the financial ladder right to the top, where financial freedom and complete chances of huge profit await you.

You can simply consider this guide-book to stand as an investment in your very own future and in all the success that awaits you. You are quite easily one of the few people who have actually taken a stand to protect your future and make something of yourself in this fast-paced and power-hungry world.

It is important for you to know that each chapter that you read through in this book will come bearing gifts in the form of tools, techniques, and guidelines that will lead you right into the arms of ultimate success, just like any other entrepreneur you are just starting. I am sure there is a lot you are not familiar with.

By reading this guide-book, you will not only gain vast knowledge, but you will see yourself looking in the eyes of secrets that you never imagined would help you reach your goals and become the best version of yourself possible.

STARTING YOUR OWN BUSINESS "SIMPLIFIED STEPS TO ENTREPRENEURIAL SUCCESS"

WHAT THIS BOOK WILL TEACH YOU

Let's take some time to jot down the things this book will help you with and open your eyes towards, especially regarding your financial freedom and entrepreneurial success. Just by skimming through the list below, I am sure you will get a good idea of just how useful of an asset this guide-book will actually stand to the for your future in the business department, so keep your eyes peeled and have a look at exactly what you are being offered here,

- Introduction into who an entrepreneur even is.
- A little bit about the work an entrepreneur even does
- Knowledge and information regarding the fears that surround the aspect of starting your own business
- Main fears of every entrepreneur
- All the information regarding the big question of, "How to start a business?"
- Strategies and plans regarding the start of your very own business
- Information on just how you can make your business a leading success.
- How exactly to achieve financial freedom?
- How to gather the perfect team for your business's success and take off.

BOOK INTRODUCTION

The dream to start off your very own business is indeed a very big one, one that often scares people. Some even tend to back out last minute because the weight of expectations and the sheer thought of failure drives them away, what a shame, losing the one thing you have the passion and potential for just on the whim of fear and hesitation.

As we have often heard the elders in our lives preach to us, *"If one is driven by success and passion, he must also be ready to accept failure as it comes."*

To be one with the dream and passion for becoming an entrepreneur in this generation and time is rather something that requires a lot of will power and trust in oneself; this is why it is good to know what you are getting into before you go for the leap of faith.

On that notice, I would like to bring it to light that, indeed, 66% of the billionaires present in the United States are self-made. If that is not enough to raise your spirits and get you going on this journey.

I would also like to inform you that at the moment there is a whopping number of 582 million entrepreneurs in the world, this means that people do succeed, granted with the right knowledge and guidance becoming a success is not really that hard!

YOUR TIME TO SHINE!

With that being said, we know to stand at the prime of what could really be your time to shine in a few years, with the right knowledge and guidance paired with the perfect team and resources there is truly no one who can stop you from becoming one of the largest self-made business and in the world.

Now you might be wondering just how this guide-book can help you open the doors to all your dreams and ultimately to a life no longer chained by financial trouble or setbacks.

Well, this book has been carefully curated and crafted to bring you the top-notch set of information and knowledge. It will guide you not only to start a business but to understand the basics of what entrepreneurial work even is. We will make sure you dive into this seemingly impossible process equipped in the best way possible, as you read on, we will discuss all the tiny details as well as the huge aspects that will lead you to your very own success.

Along with preparing you with the tools, you will need to keep your business afloat; we will also make sure you are ready to face the ups and downs that come with starting your own business. The world of business is one that revolves around money and statistics; it is easy to get crushed under larger corporations and to lose your balance.

This is why a guide-book is the perfect thing you need before you dive headfirst in a pool of sharks and a sea of other entrepreneurs all looking for the same thing as you, success.

1 WHO IS AN ENTREPRENEUR?

Before we begin stating all the techniques and keys that will help you reach entrepreneurial success. We must discuss who an entrepreneur even is; after all, it is exceptionally important actually to learn the basics of what we are diving into, and that is exactly what this chapter is all about.

Who is an entrepreneur in the first place? This is indeed the big question that we will be working on answering throughout the course of this chapter, according to the dictionary an entrepreneur is a person who sets up their own business going for the financial risks and hoping to gain profit instead of a loss.

As you read on, the idea of this will expand in your mind, and you will learn more regarding the whole topic of exactly what you will be doing and what you are going for. So, buckle up and get ready to take in as much information coming ahead as you possibly can.

The following are some wild and fairly accurate terms that have been used in the course of history to describe an ideal entrepreneur,

INITIATOR: (He is a Dreamer)
Entrepreneurs are the ones that are known to take the first and quite easily put the scariest step when it comes to starting a business. There are so many aspects that need to be considered from the very beginning.

However, there is always one person that starts the whole process and never really stops believing in it, even when things seem to slip up. Circumstances change that one person holds on even tighter and continues to work with all their heart and mind, that is the entrepreneur, the one that acts as the stronghold and the starter of the whole process.

THE LEADER, NEVER THE FOLLOWER!

The best way to put this is that the entrepreneur is indeed the leader. The one presses the start button and the one who pushes over the first domino in the grand scheme of things. He is never a follower, but rather he is the one who has a line of people following and shielding themselves behind him.

So, before you start off on the journey of initiating your very own business and standing as a leader to so many others, make sure you have the power to lead and to stand as the beginning of something truly successful and great. Make sure you are indeed the one who can stand at the frontlines.

SOMEONE WHO KNOWS HOW TO TRANSFER DREAMS INTO REALITY:

The next thing that makes a truly successful entrepreneur is a person who is truly equipped to transfer dreams into reality. Now you may be thinking this whole definition is a little vague, well to make it clearer for you and easier to understand. We will go about it in a simpler, more understandable way.

After all, at the very beginning and at the prime of everything an entrepreneur is nothing but a person with a dream, that dream is their vision, it acts as their superpower, and it is the thing that sets the rest of the business into motion, this is why when an entrepreneur sets out and works to turn that dream into something that is fairly tangible and there for you to see he is the known as the person who knows how to transfer dreams to reality.

However mostly just that is not enough, anyone can turn their dreams into a reality these days and anyone can turn a business out of their dreams, it is the aspect of success and profit that really matters here.

DREAMS TO PROFIT!

What truly matters when it comes to becoming a successful entrepreneur is the aspect of making profits off of your dreams, if you do not manage to gain profit from your dreams than all your effort goes to waste and loss is what you end up with. So, it is highly important to keep in mind that here your task is not only to transfer your dreams into reality, but rather it is to make a name for yourself and gain financial freedom; the more profit you get, the more successful you are.

ACCOUNTABILITY:

The next thing we will be discussing here is the aspect of accountability; we know that when it comes to taking the first step in something as large and risky as a business startup, there is a huge chance of failure and things going sideways. When it comes to business, once you set it up and make it public, it depends on your clients and your product to keep you afloat, there is little that you can do.

Along with the chances of success, the chances of unhappy clients and mishaps also go up, here you need to make sure you have the power of accountability for your business as well as your products.

As the initiator of the business and the mastermind behind the whole set up, it takes more than just a vision and a dream to keep an entrepreneur going. A person who owns a business also owns a large list of responsibilities that come with the ownership position; one of the main responsibilities here is that of holding yourself accountable in the face of failure.

YOUR BUSINESS COMES FIRST!

You need to make sure you know that above all else comes your business and if things do go sideways it is your job to stand up for the dream you brought to life and face the backlash, this will help maintain the face of your business and your clients will know that you are indeed a person of your word, and this business does indeed mean a lot to you. This is the point where you prove your loyalty to your work and just how worthy you are of your given position as the leader of so many.

SELF-AWARENESS:

Self-awareness is basically the phenomenon of being aware and in tune with one's own self, thoughts, actions, and behavior. A person who is self-aware is one who very rarely loses control; they are thoughtful and well maintained in all sorts of situations; this is a person who is never unsure about his/her surroundings. They remain calm and collected and almost always have a plan or course of action to follow; a self-aware person rarely loses control of a situation and is always aware of his environment.

When it comes to an entrepreneur, their job is one that comes with a lot of uncertainty and risk, with no one to look up to. An entrepreneur is indeed the one in charge of the whole operation involving the startup of a business.

This is why entrepreneurs are known to be exceptionally well contained and self-aware in order to jump into a field where failure is a threat that can strike at any moment. It requires an entrepreneur to always be on his toes and to always be aware of his surroundings.

Self-awareness stands as a key for success to an entrepreneur. The more aware they are of themselves and the things that surround them, the less they panic in the face of the stress of failure.

THE ENTREPRENEUR IS THE DRIVER:

Consider a situation like this; the entrepreneur is the driver; he is the one in the driving seat, and he is the one who is in charge of driving all his workers

and employees on top of the whole business safely.

If this person is unaware of their surroundings, they could very lead to the crash and breakdown of the whole business and the loss of their employees and workers.

This is why it is exceptionally important for the entrepreneur to know what they are doing at all costs and to be extremely self-aware.

STARTING YOUR OWN BUSINESS "SIMPLIFIED STEPS TO ENTREPRENEURIAL SUCCESS"

MINDFULNESS:

The next thing we will be discussing is indeed the aspect of mindfulness; now you may be wondering what even is mindfulness?

Well, to put it quite simply, mindfulness is the property within a human being to be fully resent in the situation and circumstance that is happening "now." It is the quality that proves that you are indeed, psychologically, and physically completely attentive in the present moment.

For an entrepreneur, this is extremely important to be aware of their surroundings and to be 100% active in the present moment. A person who is mindful has quick and sharp responses because they are not day-dreaming or lost in thoughts, but rather they are completely aware of what is going on and present; this gives them the upper hand to quickly asses every situation and reacts accordingly. An entrepreneur needs this ability in order to fight any uncertain adjustments or changes regarding their business.

You need to understand that if the owner and starter of the business are not fully present with every situation and meeting that goes on, it becomes easy for others to undermine him and take control of his very own business.

CREATIVITY:

The final thing that we will be discussing when it comes to the various characteristics found within an entrepreneur is indeed creativity. Creativity is indeed a vast topic, one that spreads onwards differently in each individual; it is the aspect that separates our work and often our aspect of thinking from everyone else in our society or environment.

Now you may be thinking, *why is it important for an entrepreneur to be creative?*

Well, an entrepreneur is after all the person who sets in motion the beginning of a new business, and in order for that business to stay afloat in a marketplace flooded by new ideas coming in every day the business needs to be creative and the person behind the business to think differently.

STARTING YOUR OWN BUSINESS "SIMPLIFIED STEPS TO ENTREPRENEURIAL SUCCESS"

What is it that highlights your business from the hundreds and thousands of other businesses, well, that is creativity! Creativity marks the glint of your thinking and personal taste that shines through in your work if you have a knack for the different things, the aspects that are not seen as much in the market we can guarantee your business will indeed be a success.

What people look for these days in a new business is something that sparks their thoughts up, something that **stands out,** this is where creativity comes in, the more creative your mind is, the more your work will stand out and the more attention it will get, the entrepreneurs that recycle already used ideas end up sinking because as it has been said so many times before, *"in order to succeed you need to do what is out of the ordinary."*

So, this is here your chance to make sure that your ideas are our own, and at the end of the day, your pattern of thinking stands out, and this will help you reach the top as you watch the look-alikes fall to the ground.

HOW WILL THIS HELP:
We have come to the end of the first chapter, and we can discuss just how the characteristics can help you with your venture regarding entrepreneurialism. We have discussed six basic personality traits and characteristics that should be present in an entrepreneur who wishes to succeed.

These are not necessarily traits that you need to be born with, but rather through practice and hard work, one can shape themselves to contain all these aspects, the more creative you are, and the further your brain goes. When it comes to ideas and dreams, the more unique your business will be, and hence it will stand out more, the more self-aware you are, the less you will feel threatened by failure and the more confident you will be.

Similarly, when you begin to take responsibility for your actions, you immediately win the hearts of your customers and clients, this shows that you are indeed worthy of leadership. Here you need to understand that all these little personality traits and characteristics may not seem as important when studied individually.

Still, when they come together, they build the perfect package of a person striving for the best.

So now that you have some knowledge regarding the type of entrepreneurs who actually make it in the business field, we can easily move on to the next chapter:

2 FEARS BEFORE STARTING A BUSINESS

When you start off in the business industry, there will be a lot of doubts that will seem to dance around your shoulders, in the beginning, people will tell you to step back before you fail and some will try to scare you away from your dreams. Still, here we need to understand that human beings often hold others back from the things they fear they are unable to do themselves. Just because other people do not have it in them does not mean your dreams should go to waste.

The key here is to never let other people's words get to you, take them as inspiration to lift you up, you have not got something to prove, and with the right work ethic and guidance, your success will stand to be proof that nothing can ever really hold a determined person back, neither is anything ever impossible for the one who truly puts in his/her all.

At the end of the day, it is up to you, if you wish to be the one who takes a risk and ends up with multitudes of success or if you wish you remain in your comfort zone peeking at your dreams wondering what it would have been like if you had actually taken a chance.

That is why, through the course of this chapter, we will be discussing all the little as well as significantly large fears that haunt your mind when you think about starting your own business.

BUCKLE UP!
It is time for you to buckle up and divert your full attention towards the knowledge you will be obtained here because we will now be discussing all the things that may be holding you back from giving your all when it comes to turning your dreams into reality.

We know that even the thought of starting your own business from scratch seems frightening. A thousand thoughts and doubts pop up in your mind, you begin to question if you are even good enough to pull this off, and that is exactly why we have compiled a list of most common fears that arise in an entrepreneur's mind.

STARTING YOUR OWN BUSINESS "SIMPLIFIED STEPS TO ENTREPRENEURIAL SUCCESS"

When it comes to starting their own business, we hope that by going through this carefully crafted list, you will understand that you are not the only one who encounters these fears. Still, rather it is completely normal to have these questionable and frightening thoughts as well as doubts regarding your work and future. But above everything else, we will make sure that you know just how to deal with these fears and not let them get to you at the end of the day.

A LIST OF FEARS THAT YOU MAY ENCOUNTER WHEN IT COMES TO STARTING YOUR OWN BUSINESS:

AM I TOO LATE IN STARTING MY BUSINESS?

The first one on our list is indeed one of the most common worries and fears that attack an entrepreneur quite often. It is the thought, and the equation of being too late, the worry of not having done anything sooner, and the fear of falling behind that haunts a lot of new entrepreneurs and even gets some to give up before they have started in the first place.

This thought is one that relates to age often. We know that 70% of entrepreneurs that begin business are in between the ages of 20-35 these numbers tend to scare off a lot of entrepreneurs who are seemingly "getting old." The other factor that contributes to this fear is the fact of an idea becoming too old. We all often have a lot going on in our minds. Ideas seem to pop up all the time.

We often even jot these ideas down and think *"this is perfect for my own business,"* but with time add responsibilities, things keep getting in the way, and we often end up forgetting to do anything about the written down idea. When we finally come back to it after all our other tasks are taken care of, we begin to worry that maybe it is indeed too late.

Well, whatever reason may bring you to think that it is too late for you to start your own business; we have come together with a few reasons that will help it this fear to rest and get you to focus on actually working towards your success.

REASONS WHY IT IS NOT TOO LATE TO START YOUR BUSINESS:

The following are some reasons that will help in raising your spirits and eliminating the fear of "being too late."

- You have gained more experience.

- The older you grow, the more people you know and the wider your business spreads. You become more mature with time, and you learn exactly how to set your goals and how to end up achieving them in the end.

- Investors begin to take you more seriously. With age comes a better understanding of money, and investors want nothing more than a person who can manage their investments.

- You have had time to experiment, and now, you know exactly what you want from life, your vision is clear, and so is your point of passion.

- With age comes the aspect of one having some savings. You are immediately more financially secure, and hence you do not risk as much.

- You have seen what failure looks like, and it is no longer a concept that is entirely new to you and that makes it less threatening.

- Self-confidence in you rises with time, age, and experience.

I DON'T HAVE SUFFICIENT MONEY:

The next point on our list is one that comes to mind of every entrepreneur,  no matter the age or experience money is something we are all afraid to lose, it is indeed the basic thing that keeps us afloat and the thought of not having enough money to start off your business.

To put it directly, this is the reason around 90% of entrepreneurs thinking of launching their business tend to back out at the last minute. It is the thought of running out of all your e=assets and failing then going into bankruptcy that drives them away from going through with starting their own business.

This is the fear that is inevitable and the most realistic one on our list because it is indeed true, in this world without money no one really makes it, and if you feel you are already low on assets the risk begins to seem too big, and it pushes you to back off.

CONSIDER OTHER MEANS OF FUNDING:

Starting a business, the money needed to start everything off usually comes from the savings of the entrepreneur. This is where the scary thing comes because if this venture leads to failure, then it can very well mean the loss of all the assets and money put into the business in the beginning.

The best practice to get over this fear is to make sure that all the money you will be investing in your business is not coming straight out of our pocket, but rather before you embark on this journey make sure you have other means of funding too, for example,

- Loans from banks
- Loans from family members
- Looking for reliable investors

- You must look for an alternate form of funding in order to get rid of the fear that you may not have enough money to start off your own business.

FEAR OF REJECTION:

Rejection is, by far, one of the greatest fears we come to face as we grow in life and start to take steps towards a better, brighter future. *Now you may be wondering, what does the fear of rejection even mean in the first place?*

Basically, the fear of rejection is known as an irrational fear that leads you to believe that whatever work you do will not be accepted or appreciated by people. Rather they will feel negative about it, and this fear makes you draw back from living out your dreams, *"what will people think?"* is a phrase that ends up taking away dreams from far too many.

When it comes to this particular fear, there is one thing that matters the most, and that is the way you think and perceive things around you, it is your perception that can either save you from this irrational fear or it can be the cause of your downfall. What I mean, when I say this is that, it is entirely up to you whether you decide that to accept the fact that from the beginning to the end of your journey.

Every person or client or company you indulge will not completely stand by your work, or like your work, this is quite frankly impossible. We all live in an environment full of different people from different backgrounds and patterns of thinking; their likes and dislikes are all different from one another. We can never expect everyone to agree with us or to support our business.

The solution to getting over this fear is to know in your heart that there will always be someone who does not approve of your work, but this does not mean that there won't be people who absolutely adore it too.

I DO NOT HAVE AN EXPERIENCE OR EDUCATION:

One fear that seems too often haunt entrepreneurs who are just starting up is that they do not have a high level of education or experience. They feel as if without the correct amount of experience and education, their business might not be as successful, and this drives them away from ever, even giving it a proper try.

KNOWLEDGE OVER A COLLEGE DEGREE:

The first and foremost point you need to understand here is that when it comes to a business, a college degree begins to have little value, the one thing that comes above having a college degree has the knowledge, for a business you need to be aware of your surroundings, how to deal with investors and clients, etc.

A college degree will not help you as much as knowledge of the world will.

The same goes for the experience; with time and age, the experience will build up, but again the best place to start gaining experience and knowledge both is to take the first step and have faith in yourself.

This is where you need to brush off the worries of not having a piece of paper in the form of a degree and rather bring your focus towards human relations and businesses in order for you to succeed.

THE FEAR OF TAKING RISKS:

The next fear on our list is a rather important one when it comes to business and especially the start of business at the hands of an entrepreneur. As we discussed above in the previous chapter it is a really important characteristic for an entrepreneur to be able to take risks, the whole concept of entrepreneurship revolves around the idea of taking risks and going for the leap of faith without knowing how it is even going to go.

But it is always easier said than it is ever done, when it comes to actually go for taking a risk people to seem to back out, fear overtakes their passion and they simply think they cannot afford the cost that failure comes bearing. Risks can only go two ways either they end with complete success or end up drowning you out.

But in order to help you in overcoming this fear, we have come up with a list of advantages that come with taking risks going for the harder option instead of selling in comfort.

ADVANTAGES OF TAKING RISKS:
You will not have to wonder "what if" in the future if you take the risk now Risks are a highly integral part of innovation and success.

If you don't take risks, you don't move forward. Rather you find yourself stuck in the same space. Risks prove just how passionate you are about your business and just how much you are willing to give up; they show your dedication and commitment.

If all goes well, the risk you take may just end up being the best decision you've made for yourself.

So, take the risk. Without it, you will never really know the outcome, and no one ever wishes to live a life of regret. Keep in mind to face whatever comes your way, whether that be failure or success.

FINANCIAL OBLIGATIONS:

The one thing that has proven to drown entrepreneurs dream faster than anything else is the fear of not fulfilling all financial obligations that come with the prospect of starting one's own business. It is clear that so many people have heads full of ideas and passion, too, for that matter, but the one area that ends up killing their determination and holding them back is indeed the hassle of financial obligations.

We know that when an entrepreneur starts out, he/she needs the business to set off on the base of their very own income that often comes out of their pocket, and as scary as it seems in the wake of failure, they can lose every last penny.

It is the fear of losing everything at the end of the day that holds so many of us back, but what if someone were to tell you that on the other side if you succeed the amount you gain will be so much more than what you invest, and it is often the thought of profit that keeps so many of us going. So, this is where the challenge seems to stand, are you willing to get everything you have to either fly or sink is completely up to you.

Ultimately, it depends on the passion you have and how far you are willing to go.

However, before you can go about making that decision, you need to understand what these financial obligations even are in the first place.

FINANCIAL OBLIGATIONS OF AN ENTREPRENEUR:

- Investing in a start-up
- Paying employees
- Insurance costs
- Start-up notification
- Taxation
- The following are some responsibilities that fall on the shoulders of entrepreneurs when they are starting out, but when success comes, it all does truly seem worth it!

So, read on! As we progress further in the journey of helping you achieve a successful business along with reaching the ultimate goal of financial freedom, watch things come together as we proceed. Hopefully, the knowledge you obtain here will be of a lot of use when it comes to practical life and managing a business of your very own.

3 HOW TO START A BUSINESS

We can now move on to the prospect of actually starting your very own business, as we have taken a good amount of time above to make sure that you feel ready and equipped to begin this risky journey, that is the main reason we decided to discuss all the characteristics and personality traits on top of the various fears that you might collide with on the way to starting your very own business and becoming an entrepreneur, it is never easy at the start nut with time and experience things start to go smoother, after all, you must begin somewhere in order to reach success.

In this chapter we will be discussing the basics of starting your very own business, we will list down all the various strategies one needs to get going, and all the techniques that keep the business afloat when things begin to go sideways. When it comes to starting a business, you need to start off with a strong mindset, inspiration, and the will to keep going even when you realize you might actually end up failing.

The start of business feels like the first day of school. You do not really know if the others will accept you, you're unfamiliar with your surroundings and comfort seems like a blessing too far out of reach at this point, we all know the feeling of being uneasy and lost, this is the time where your passion, motivation, and knowledge saves you from backing out at the last minute.

WHAT DOES IT TRULY MEAN TO START BUSINESS?

Before we discuss the techniques, you will need to start your very own business. We need to make sure you actually understand what you are in for here. Starting a business of your own is more than just a group of investments and a source of income, with your business comes a large level of responsibility. You are in charge of not just yourself and your actions but also the work and actions of all the people you recruit.

Eventually, a lot of other people's income, a daily form of survival, will depend on you. You need to make sure every step you take is one that is taken with caution and thought.

Starting a business is never just about you, but rather it is more about the people. Still, rather the ones you serve, the clients, the day you start your business off your life becomes one of putting your own self last and others before you, so the sacrifice is one best thing you should always keep in mind.

The other thing you need to keep in mind is that things do not always go your way, with an easy-going mindset and accepting the smaller failures you will be able to focus more on the bigger picture and once you stop stressing over what is not necessary you will see success coming your way.

ALL YOU NEED TO KNOW ABOUT STARTING YOUR OWN BUSINESS:

Read on as we discuss all the various techniques you will need to start off your own business and lead yourself into financial independence and freedom, after all. So, we suggest you pay close attention to the points below as they may just end up serving you in more ways than you could ever even imagine, these tools and techniques may go on to be the vital bases of your success in the business industry.

1. DEVELOP A BUSINESS MARKETING PLAN:

A business marketing plan is quite frankly the first thing you should have at hand just when you even begin to think about going for a business venture of your own, without a plan you will never really have a way of knowing what you want to achieve and that will lead you to your downfall.

What is a business marketing plan?

So, a business marketing plan is basically an outline of what you wish to achieve from your business, more than that it shows what type of a strategy you will be adapting to market your business and get the word out about it. It is known to be a template or an overview that shows an insight into all your marketing strategies as well as goals.

The following are some things a business plan is known to highlight:

- **Overall summary of the business model:**

This should summarize what your business is about and what you hope to achieve from this venture, it should be to the point and easy to understand.

- **A strategy to follow strictly:**

Once you have come up with a summary of your goals, the next thing to do here is to come up with a reliable strategy and to make sure you can follow the said strategy in order to reach your goals.

- **Availability of product as well as the services:**

You also need to make sure before you go on with taking your business public that you have a reasonable number of products, so you do not end up running out and disappointing your clients.

- **A timeline for all tasks and goals to be completed:**

It is crucial for all entrepreneurs to have a timeline for each of your tasks and goals, this will help you stay on track and prevent you from falling behind on the aspect of achieving your goals, it will also keep you alert.

2. A STRATEGY: FULFILL YOUR PASSION:

Once you succeed in building the perfect business plan, the next thing you need to bring your attention towards is making sure you do not end up losing your passion along the way. This indeed happens to a large number of entrepreneurs.

They start out with this fire in their heart. Still, after some time the statics and financials and all other aspects end up making them dull, there is truly nothing worse than losing one's passion in life, they say the day a person loses his passion in life is the day he begins to see the world in black and white instead of color.

So, this is why we have decided to discuss just how you can go about the business world without losing your passion.

The following are some ways you can continue to work and go after success all the while having the same passion in your heart:

- **Remain surrounded by creativity:**

We know that creativity is the one thing that fuels passion in life, so make sure when you set out to start your business, the people you employ and the ones you spend your time around are just as creative and passionate as you.

- **Keep taking feedback from others:**

Another really great way to continue with passion and inspiration is to take other's criticism and always look for ways to improve yourself.

- **Never forget why you started out doing what you are doing now:**

the best way of keeping yourself afloat and preventing yourself from losing your passion when it comes to business is to continuously remind yourself of why you started out in the first place, and this will stop the fire within your heart from going out as you will continuously be reminded of the things that truly matter in life.

3. Availability of products and services:

The next big thing on our wish-list is the aspect of making sure you the required amounts of products and resources to set off your business. This is the aspect that ensures that you never fall short when it comes to business and directly dealing with your clients.

Products, we mean, the items your business revolves around. At the end of the day, it is what the client has come to you for, and no matter how good your people are and your marketing strategies are if you simply are unable to provide the product the client has come to you for. It not only ruins the reputation of your business but risks your work to go into loss.

Summarily, if you have the perfect product in stock and a line of clients waiting to get their hands on it, but you run out of staff it causes a huge mishap, with no one to guide the clients the end up going towards other business and this leads you into a loss.

4. PRICING STRATEGIES:

What you price you choose to sell your product on has a huge impact on  the number of customers and clients you get as well as the overall reputation of your business. As we have discussed before, as the days go by, more and more business with new strategies seem to be popping up, the competition is at an all-time time high, and that is why you need to be very thorough and always have a close look on your products price range.

You need to understand that as a new business in the market you cannot just begin selling your products at a really high price, this will just end up driving your customers away, and what you need to be doing here is setting prices that draw clients towards you, when you work up a strong pricing strategy it causes the customers to actually want to engage with your product.

5. WHO WILL GET BENEFITS FROM YOUR BUSINESS:

Once you have the pricing strategies in line, the next step you need to bring your focus towards is the question of who will even benefit from this business of mine? As we discussed above, the day you begin your very own business is the day it stops being about you but rather begins to revolve around the clients.

The investors and the employees, you need to learn to put the ones contributing to your dream first and make sure that they get their share of income from your success as without them none of it would have ever been possible.

The benefits of your business are mostly in the form of income. You need to be able to ivied them equally. At the end of the day, the more the income is, the more you will benefit, this will not only bring an excellent reputation to your company it will also help you gain more investors to continue your mission towards success.

6. SHORT TERM AND LONG-TERM OBJECTIVES:

One of the key aspects that you need to sort out before you set off on starting your very own business is to manage a list of long term and short-term objectives. These are the things that can help you to achieve, and they serve as the driving force behind your success. They help you remain focused on what is essential.

The short-term goals are the ones you achieve in a single go, and you know that is achieved by one large action and force of work. However the long term goals are the ones that remain with you over time, you put work into them constantly little by little they begin to build up and as time passes and more and more effort is put into them they provide you with a huge source of income and success.

You need to keep on mind that these goals are meant to come together over time, and they are the key to the success of your business, they are a list and a summarization of all that you need to achieve with your business, and they help when it comes to keeping you on track at the end of the day.

7. SWOT ANALYSIS

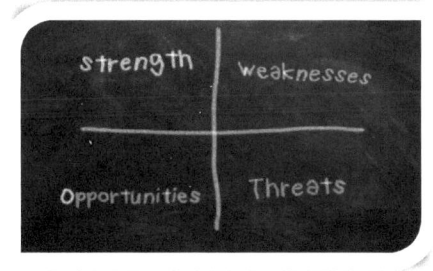

The final thing on our list is the factor of SWOT analysis. This is basically a technique used by companies and businesses to help identify their strengths, weaknesses as well as the opportunities they need to grab hold of. It is a thought out of a strategic plan that helps them know their strengths and the things they are weak in better. This plan also consists of threats that the company may think they can face in the future along with the competition they have regarding other companies of the same kind.

The SWOT analysis is by far the best method to prepare yourself before you jump into the world of business as it puts before you all the things you seem to be good at and the ones you need to work on as well as the ones you need to protect yourself against, the whole plan is best described as,

- **S**trengths: the things in your business that are considered to be advantages and can lead you to success.
- **W**eaknesses: the aspects regarding your business that may end up causing your downfall, the things you further need to work on.
- **O**pportunities: this is a heads up for all the things you need to be looking out for in the form of opportunities that will be good for your business
- **T**hreats: these are the things you need to preserve protection against and be very careful of as they stand as threats to the growth and success of your business.

4 HOW TO MAKE YOUR BUSINESS SUCCESSFUL

Now that we have reached the final chapter, it is time for us to discuss the final aspect when it comes to starting your very own business. Once you have a good idea of all the little things you need to get in order and your goals, as well as procedures, are completed.

You are officially ready to start your business off. The next thing you need to worry about is the actual success of the business.

That is exactly what we will be discussing here, the final step to the perfect business being learning the strategies needed to reach success, so read on as this knowledge will defiantly help you reach your dreams as an entrepreneur.

STEPS TO MAKE YOUR BUSINESS A SUCCESS!

The following is a list of steps that will help you in your journey towards success as an entrepreneur.

FIND PEOPLE WHO ARE FIT FOR THE JOB:

We know that without employees, our business has no way of staying afloat, these are the people who directly interact with your clients. Some who work behind the scenes to manage your company's tech as well as finances.

When it comes to starting a business, you are never really on your own, and the people you pick to help you manage your business have a huge hand in its success or downfall.

CHOOSE WISELY:

So, this is where we warn you to choose wisely, conduct interviews, and review the CVs of the people you call for hiring. Make sure that each person that is directed toward a job can even manage it and will not let you down.

Once you have the perfect team of people working for you, your business will no longer be at risk of falling apart at the hand of the ones you have hired to keep it going.

If you end up hiring people who are not trained in the areas they need to work in it will cause mishaps and even unhappy clients and that is pretty much the last thing a new business needs with all the competition already present in the market these days, you need people who are really good at what they do at all costs!

EACH TEAM MEMBER MUST BE DETERMINED:
Once you succeed in hiring the right people for the jobs required to be done, the next thing you need to worry about is the enthusiasm and mindset of the people who you are going to be working with.

Assembling a team of people to work with you in the process of bringing a whole new business to its feet can be a hard job, the people you work with must be aware of what they are in for; they must be educated and willing to stand by your side through all the ups and downs.

All of these people must have the determination and motivation to keep something like a new business running. The ones around you, the team you are supposed to be counting on, simply remain unmotivated. It affects the way even you begin to view your business, and instead of bringing you together, it ends up tearing your whole team apart.

Before you hire the people on your team, make sure that they are just as passionate and willing to make this business a success as you and will not let minor setbacks affect them greatly but will rather work even harder in the face of a threat or failure.

EACH TEAM MEMBER HAS A BARRIER-BREAKING CAPACITY:

What we mean when we say that each team member present beside you need to have barrier-breaking authority is that the communication between the bosses and employees should be clear cut and strong.

This means that the authorities would have a good understanding of the people working underneath them in smaller positions, and the ones in the said smaller positions should also have clear goals and objectives along with great communication strategies.

These are the little things that prevent hassle in your business when the authorities and the people above are on good relations with the ones working for them the face front of your company becomes exceptionally strong you begin to fearless as nothing can really tear you apart before you begin to worry about outward threats you need to take a look on the inside and make sure the people working for you are on good relations and have a good method of communication with each other.

The next thing you need to make sure is that the people you put in your team as a member has the dedication and power to take charge when every single person working for you is capable of taking risks and doesn't fear much it becomes impossible for threats to actually affect you and that is exactly what you need in order to reach success.

ENERGIZE THE TEAM:
Now that we have talked about the individual efforts and characteristics required to be present in each team member. we need to move on to talk about the collective team as a whole and the things you need to look out for when educating your team members before taking your business public and allowing them to directly interact with your clients.

SHARED PURPOSE:
The first thing that your team needs to be aware of is the factor of shared purpose. You need to educate them about the true reason they are even working in the first place, make them see that one goal that brings them to work every day, it is indeed the success of this business.

Once they become familiar with the main purpose of their work, you need to make them understand that after all, the people they work with share the same goals, and hence working together ends up being the only way they can achieve that one huge goal of theirs.

When they see that they are all putting in efforts for the same single purpose, they will begin to combine their efforts, and this will provide unity and strength in your team, which is the perfect combination for success.

ATTENTION TOWARDS REALITY:

This is where you need to make the people working with you and for you were aware of the reality of starting a business and being a part of something as huge and risky as a new business. They say that expectations seem to be the reason you face the biggest downfalls, so make sure that the people working for you have realistic expectations.

The goals they have set should not be completely impossible to reach, but rather more towards reality. This will help them remain grounded and focused instead of having them work towards goals they will never be able to achieve at the end of the day.

COVERT DREAMS TO MILESTONES & MOBILIZE HEARTS & MINDS:

Now that we have discussed a great deal about the people you will pick to work with you in your quest to reach financial freedom and build a business that stands successfully on its feet. You need to bring your goals and ideas in one place and convert them to milestones, instead of just having ideas in your head or a vision.

You need to start taking the success of your company and business more seriously; the one way to do this is to take a look at the goals you have set for yourself.

As an entrepreneur who is just starting out you must have a lot of ideas and creative goals regarding your business some even may be considered as unrealistic by other and some may be really hard to achieve just at the beginning, there is a certain excitement to starting your very own business, but this is the time you need to actually focus on a strategy to keep you grounded and to make sure you actually end up achieving all these goals of yours.

Milestones will help build a map leading you to success, as you start out to make sure to put the rather smaller easier ones first. With time they will grow, so will your knowledge and willpower and before you know it the most difficult of your dreams will be coming true as the milestones continue to go into completion, it is a safe process to help ensure that you stay on track and do not lose sight of the reason you started out in the first place.

BUILD SOLID RELATIONSHIPS:

One of the most important things when it comes to a business and the people you work with is the kind of relationship you have with them. When it comes to working, the relationships you have with the people you work with and work for need to be carefully maintained as these are indeed the people that are helping you keep your dream alive.

The first thing you need to make sure here is that the relationships you have with the people working for you and alongside you are not pressurized, let them build with time, and have trust in your people forced relationships end up being hollow. They fall apart with the passage of time.

COMMUNICATION:

The main thing that will lead you to the best and strongest type of relationship with your team members is the factor of communication. This is the one thing that will ensure that your people understand each other better and come face to face with their problems, it will help eliminate any friction in relations and ultimately lead your relations to become solid, which is the perfect mix for a business that is just starting out in a large industry with so many competitors.

So, make sure that the relations between the people you rely on to run your business are solid and will not falter at the hands of threats, the more unity between your people, the stinger your front will be.

ACHIEVE FINANCIAL FREEDOM:

And the final goal on our list tends to be the most important one. When it comes to achieving financial freedom, there are a lot of things you need to make sure are in line first, risks you have to take, and even threats you have to face.

Still, at the end of the day, it is all really worth it because you no longer have the burden n financials on your back, and you can completely bring your focus towards your business without fear.

Achieving financial freedom seems to be the final point of success when it comes to your business, once you have the right amount of knowledge.

You begin to put in all the work needed into your business you will see how your profit will begin to increase, with time your profit will overcome the amount you spent on investments and from there on out it is just financial freedom for you.

The following is a list of things you need to keep in mind before you think of achieving financial freedom.

- Have all your goals in order and in the form of millstones
- Track all the money you spend on your business including the investments you make
- Pay all your debts off before you out any earnings to your pocket
- Pay yourself fairly and first
- Know where you stand and where you need to be, stay aware of your progress rate
- Set goals for financial independence
- Hire someone to look through your financials and offer you professional advice
- Financial freedom seems to be the ultimate goal of almost every entrepreneur who starts off. With time, the effort of the correct knowledge just about anything is possible. You just need to have trust in yourself and your business.

Once you reach financial freedom, things indeed become a tad bit easier, and life around you begin to settle. So, remember to have patience as great things await you based on the work that you put in and the trust you keep within yourself and the ones working alongside you.

BOOK SUMMARY

Here we stand!

Yes! We have indeed reached the ending of our journey filled with knowledge, information, strategies, and procedures that have solely been picked and put together for the success of your entrepreneurial success.

Each chapter has been layered with the knowledge to help you and guide you in the simplest and easiest ways possible.

We are aware that starting out in the world of business is as if you are about to dive into an ocean of sharks, here you will not be able to survive for long without the correct knowledge and guidance, and this is why we decided to put to together the perfect e-book, containing all the little things that will equip you for the journey of risks and decision making ahead.

TAKE A LEAP OF FAITH!

As you have now read through the book designed to help entrepreneurs start with confidence and courage, you must feel as if you are well equipped to take a leap of faith now, what better time to begin working on making your dreams a reality than when you have all the knowledge to guide you by your side.

It is indeed your turn to take the first step now, with your goals and dreams in the order it is time for you to set off on the prime of your entrepreneurial journey. Hopefully, nothing but success in the form of financial freedom, as well as remarkable growth in your business, is all that awaits you on the other side.

It has been an honor to conduct this short information book to guide you on your business venture in the best way possible.

Thank you for reading this book and purchasing, I really appreciate it. If you enjoy it/find it useful then please consider leaving a review on Amazon. I am very excited and looking forward to reading each review!

Thank you

Christopher Fletcher

ABOUT THE AUTHOR

Christopher Fletcher PHD, MBA and a 27-year-old entrepreneur whom has achieved great success along his journey. His intuition, acquisition and business mind whom enjoys financial freedom.

He is a Proud American Christian who defines himself as Religious. He has a degree and PhD in Business and Economics.

He has consulted for hundreds of start-up businesses and is a principal of Innovative Growth as an advisor.

He grew up in a middle-class neighborhood. He was raised by his father; his mother having left when he was young.

Christopher Fletcher holds a PhD in strategic management from the University of Michigan and an MBA from LA State University.

Christopher Fletcher has taught strategic management, entrepreneurship, business ethics, and entrepreneurial consulting around the globe across many institutes and commercial firms.

Christopher Fletcher wishes to pass on his wealth of knowledge and prepare you for your entrepreneur journeys.

www.ingramcontent.com/pod-product-compliance
Lightning Source LLC
Chambersburg PA
CBHW040251220526
45473CB00001B/447